# Beautiful Flowers
## Coloring Book

An Adult Coloring Book Featuring Exquisite Flower Bouquets and Arrangements for Stress Relief and Relaxation

Copyright 2019 © Coloring Book Cafe

All Rights Reserved.

**Copyright @ 2019 Coloring Book Cafe**
**All Rights Reserved.**

*All rights reserved. No part of this publication may be reproduced or used in any form or by any means-- graphic, electronic, or mechanical, including photocopying, recording, or information storage-and-retrieval-- without permission of the publisher.*

*The designs in this book are intended for the personal, noncommercial use of the retail purchaser and are under federal copyright laws; they are not to be reproduced in any form for commercial use. Permission is granted to photocopy content for the personal use of the retail purchaser.*

an Imprint of **The Fruitful Mind Publishing LTD.**
www.coloringbookcafe.com

Have questions? Let us know.
**support@coloringbookcafe.com**

# BONUS

*Relax And Create Your Own Masterpiece With*
**THIS 30 PAGE FREE** *Beautiful Adult Coloring Book*

*Claim Your FREE Coloring Book at:*

***www.freecoloringbooklet.com***

# Flower List

01 - *Peonies*

02 - *Dahlias*

03 - *Syngonium, Platicerium, Plectranthus verticillatus*

04 - *Daffodils, Bluebells (Hyacinthoides), Virginia blue bells, Wild rose,*

05 - *Lilies*

06 - *Sunflowers*

07 - *Astromelia*

08 - *Poppies*

09 - *Roses*

10 - *Petunias*

11 - *Hibiscus*

12 - *Sansevieria trifasciata, Maranta*

13 - *Succulents mix*

14 - *Cacti mix*

16 - *Hydrangea*

16 - *Asplenium Fern, Chlorophytum comosum (Spider plant)*

17 - *Dwarf palmetto, Canna lily*

18 - *Oxalis*

19 - *Potted Geranium*

20 - *Chinese Money Plant, African Violets*

21 - *Sunflowers*

22 - *Roses, and wild roses*

23 - *Tulips*

24 - *Campanula isophylla (Italian bell flower)*

25 - *Alcea rosea hollyhock*

*Peonies*

# Dahlias

# Syngonium, Platicerium, Plectranthus verticillatus

*Virginia Blue Bells, Wild Rose*

*Lilies*

*Sunflowers*

*Astromelia*

*Poppies*

# Roses

*Petunias*

*Hibiscus*

# Sansevieria Trifasciata, Maranta

*Succulents Mix*

*Cacti Mix*

*Hydrangea*

*Asplenium Fern, Chlorophytum comosum (Spider plant)*

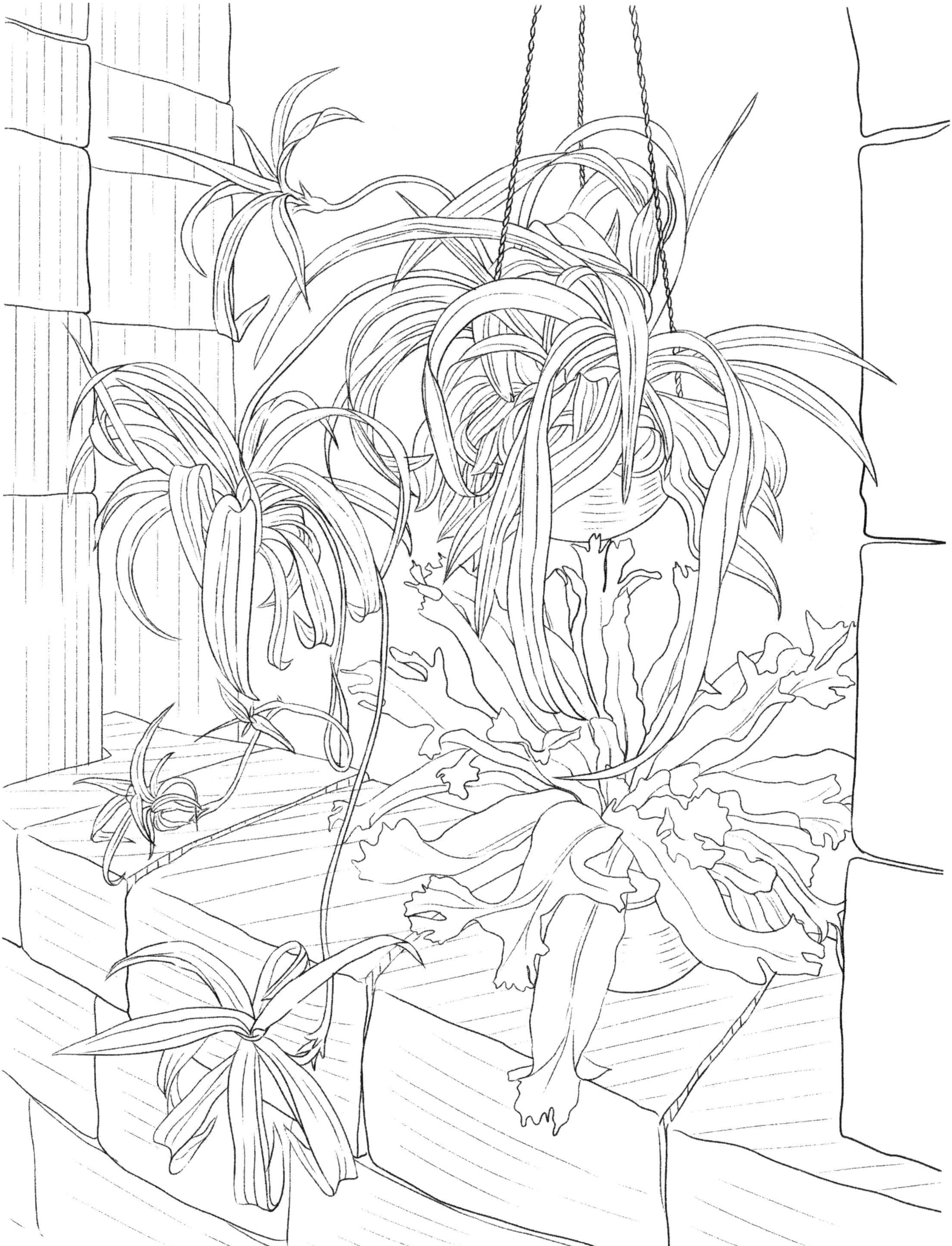

# Dwarf Palmetto, Canna Lily

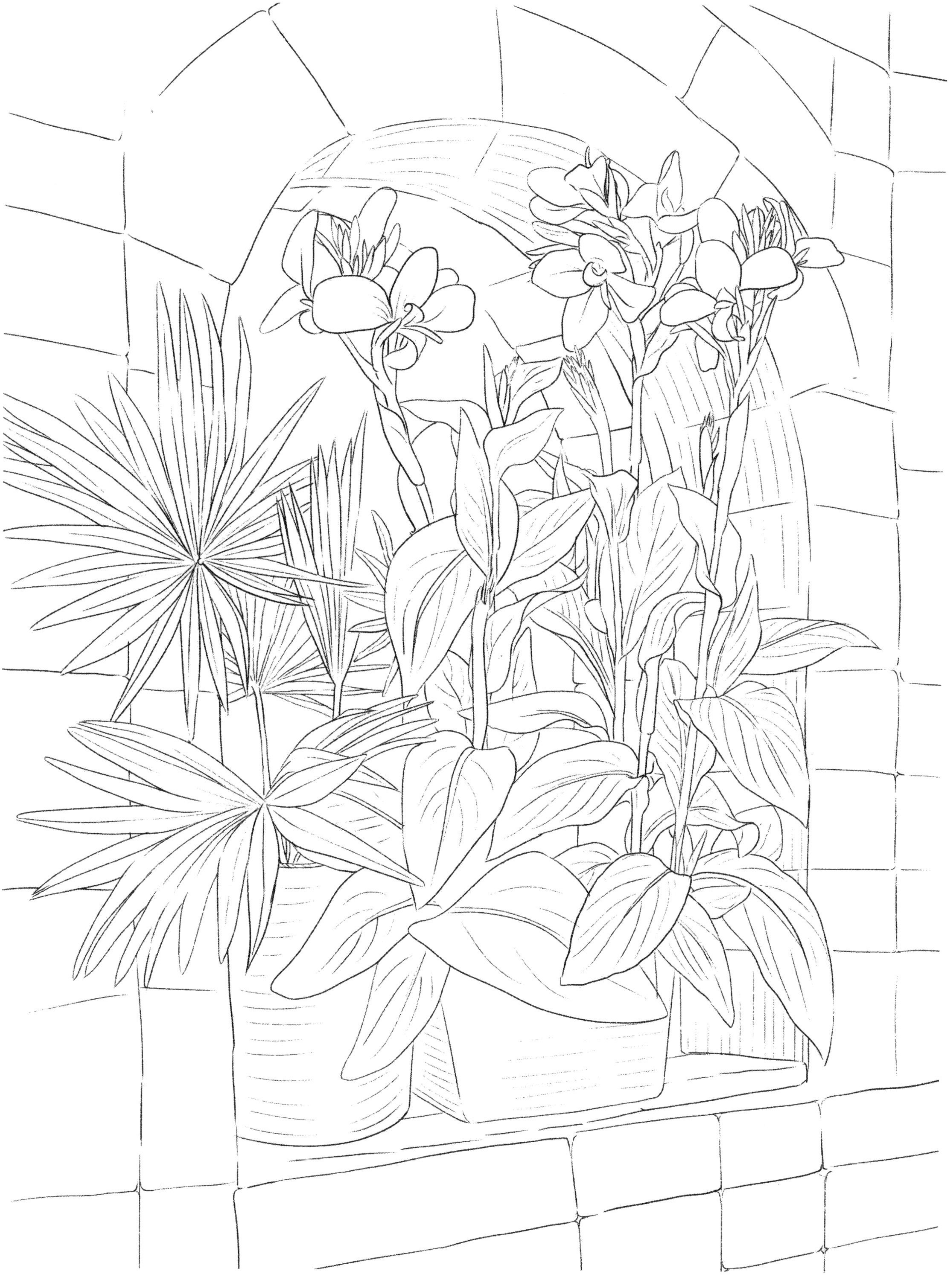

*Oxalis*

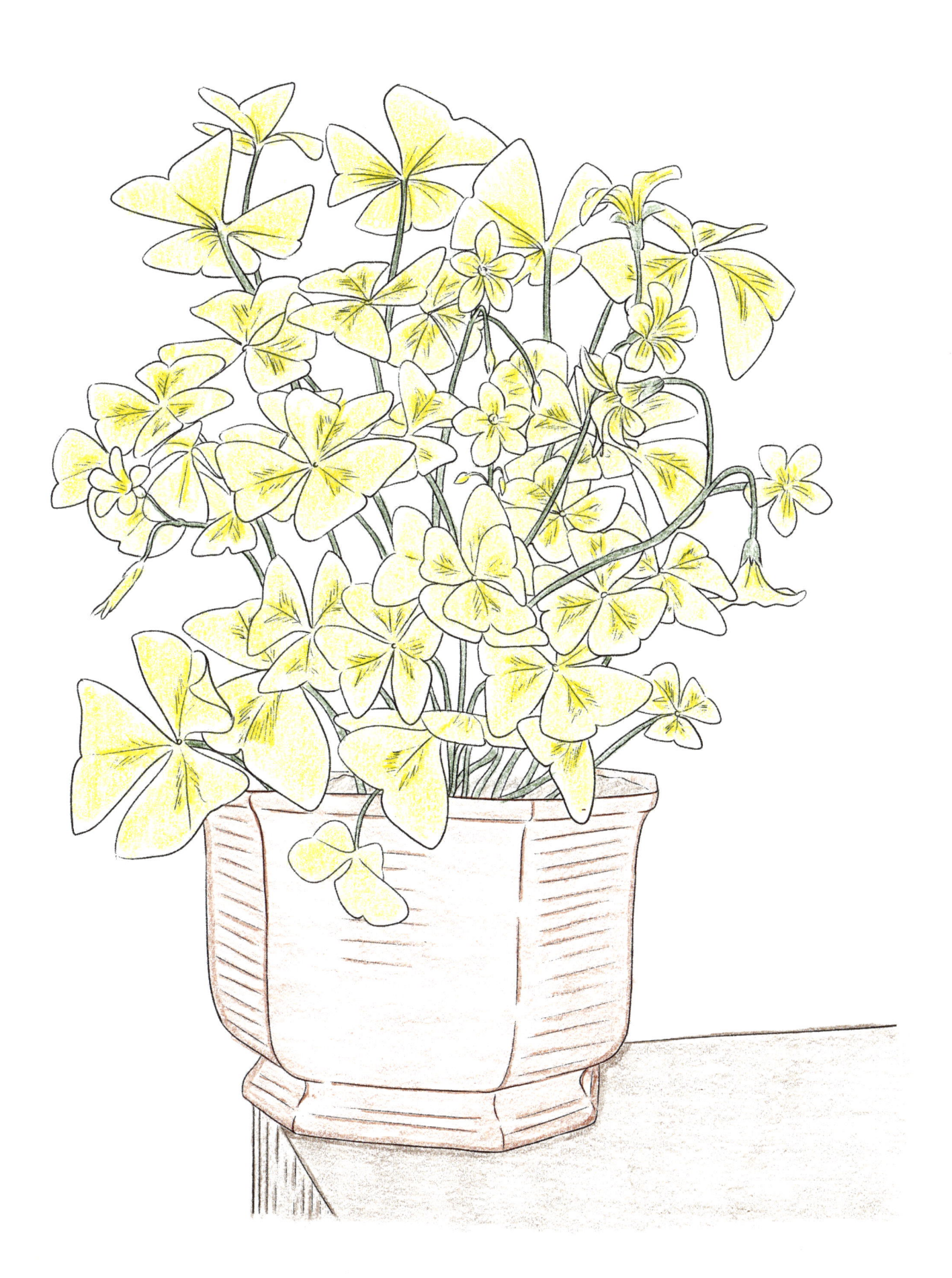

Potted Geranium

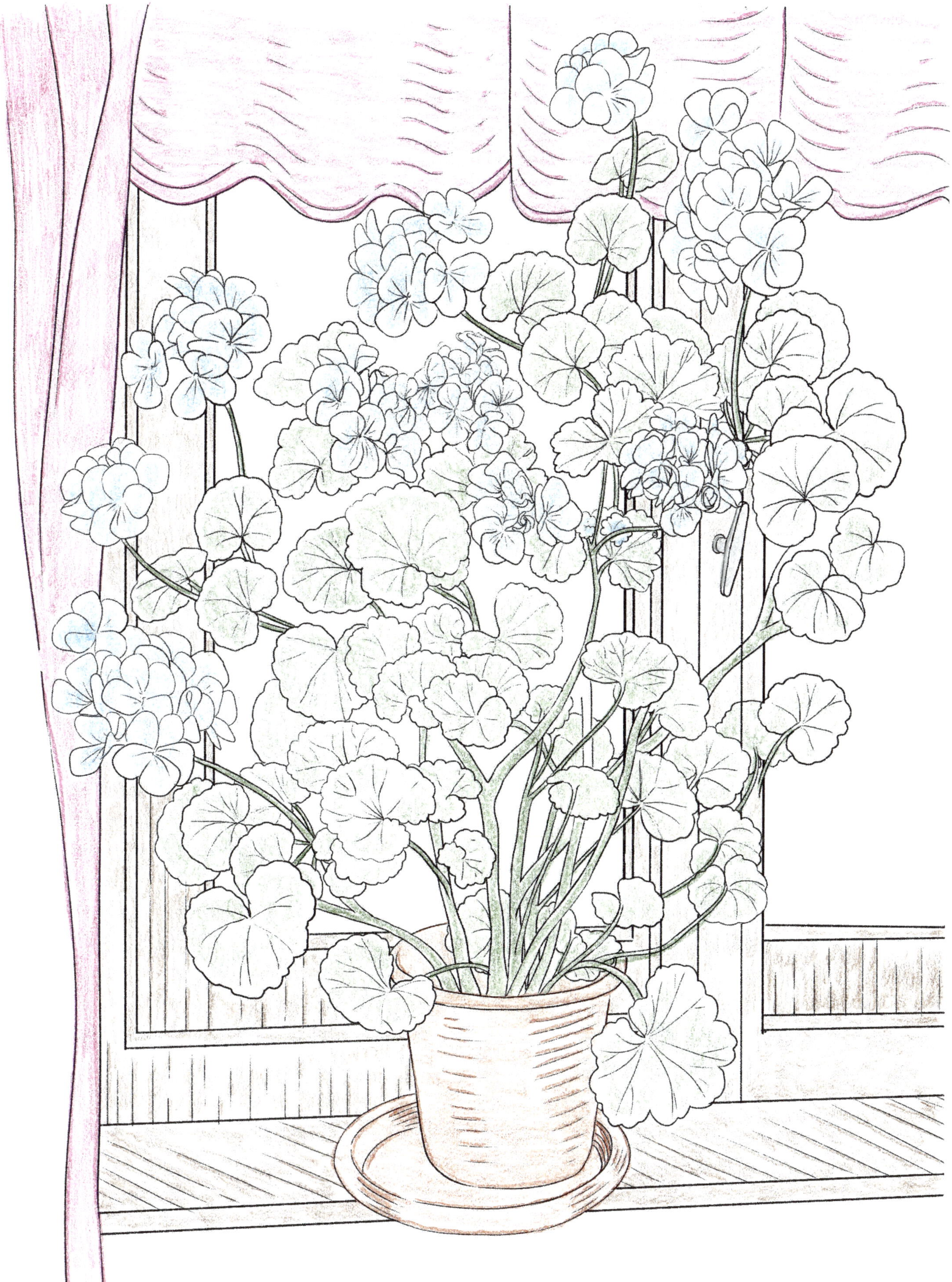

*Chinese Money Plant,
African Violets*

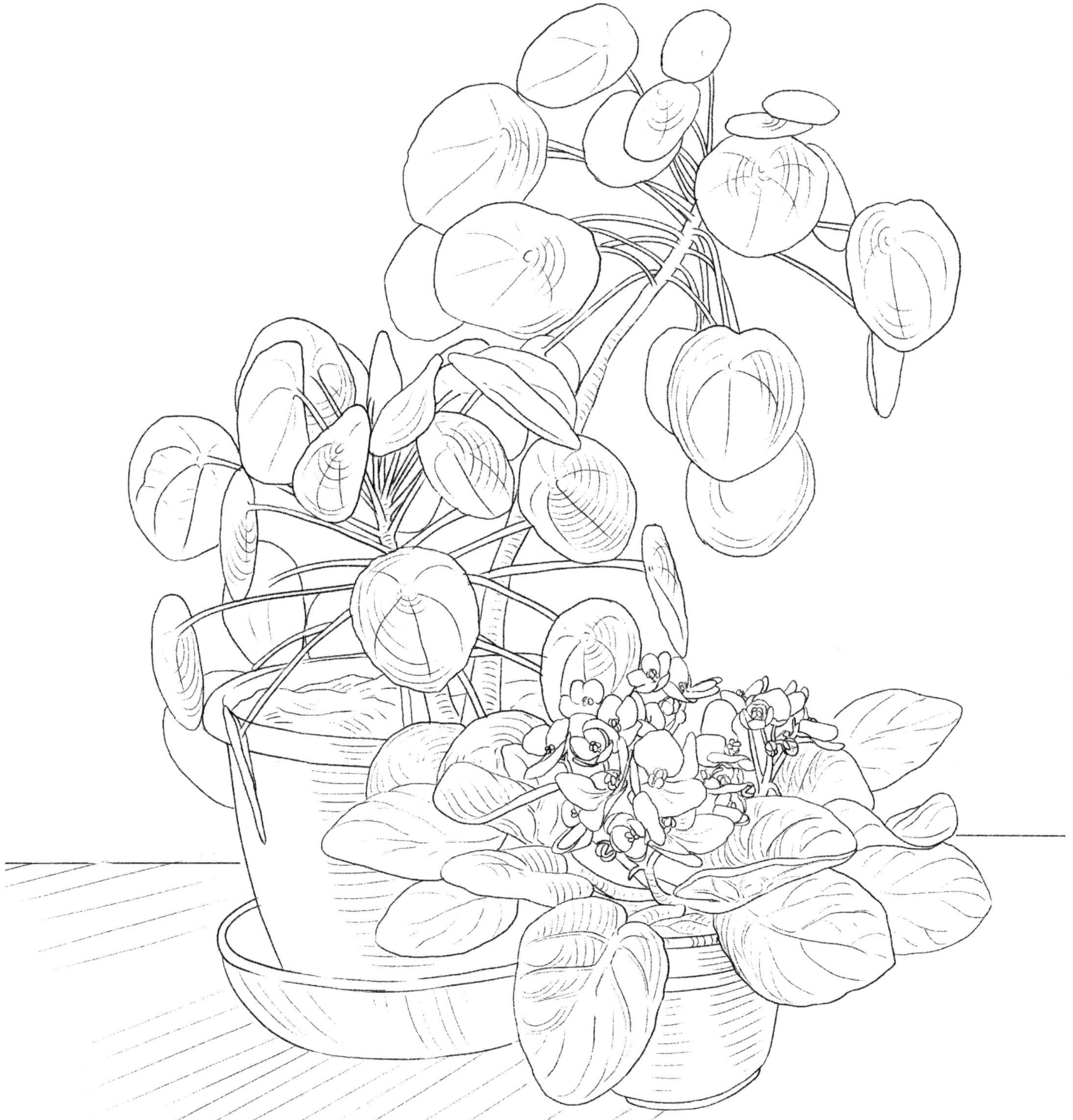

*Sunflowers*

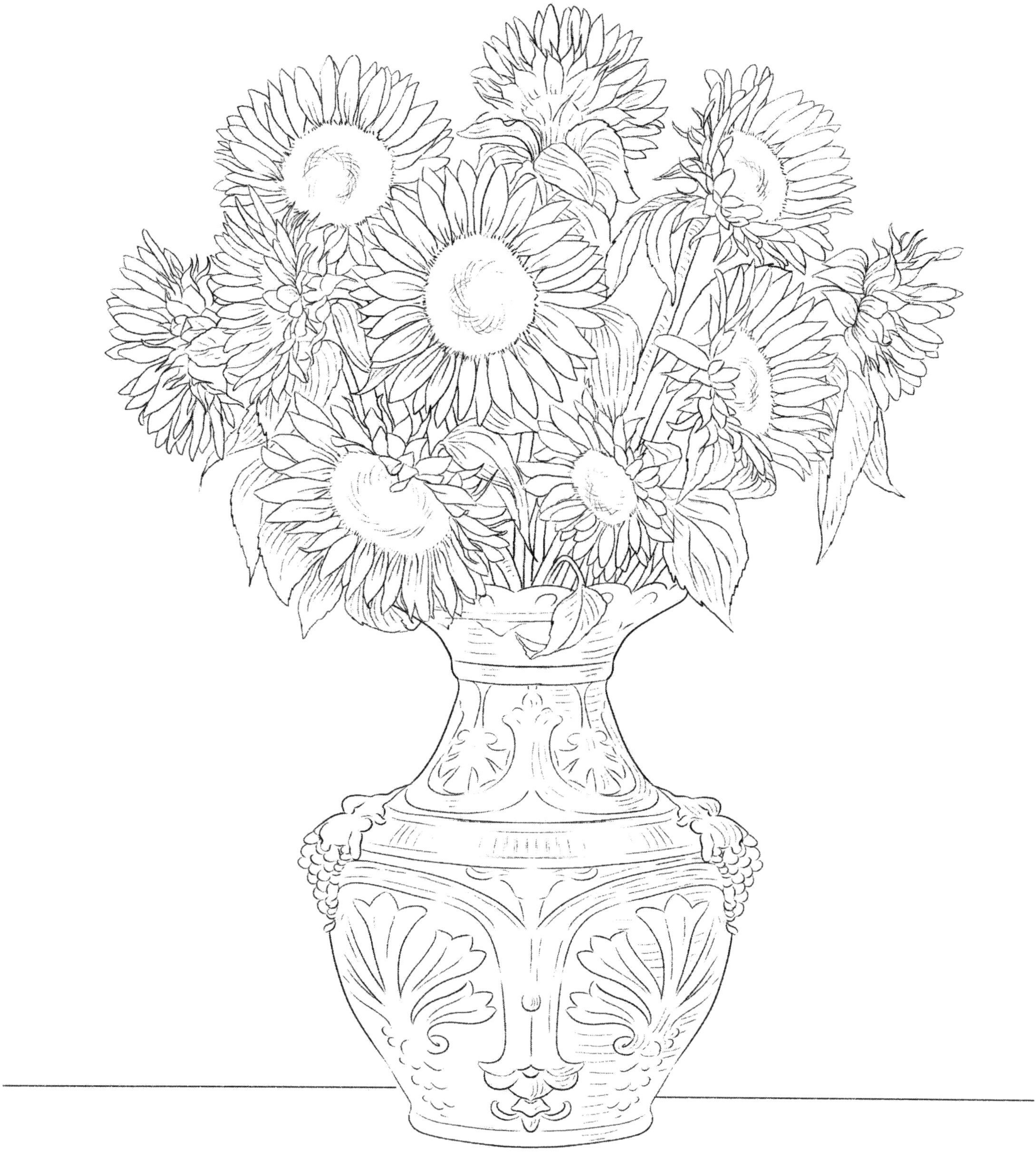

# Roses, and Wild Roses

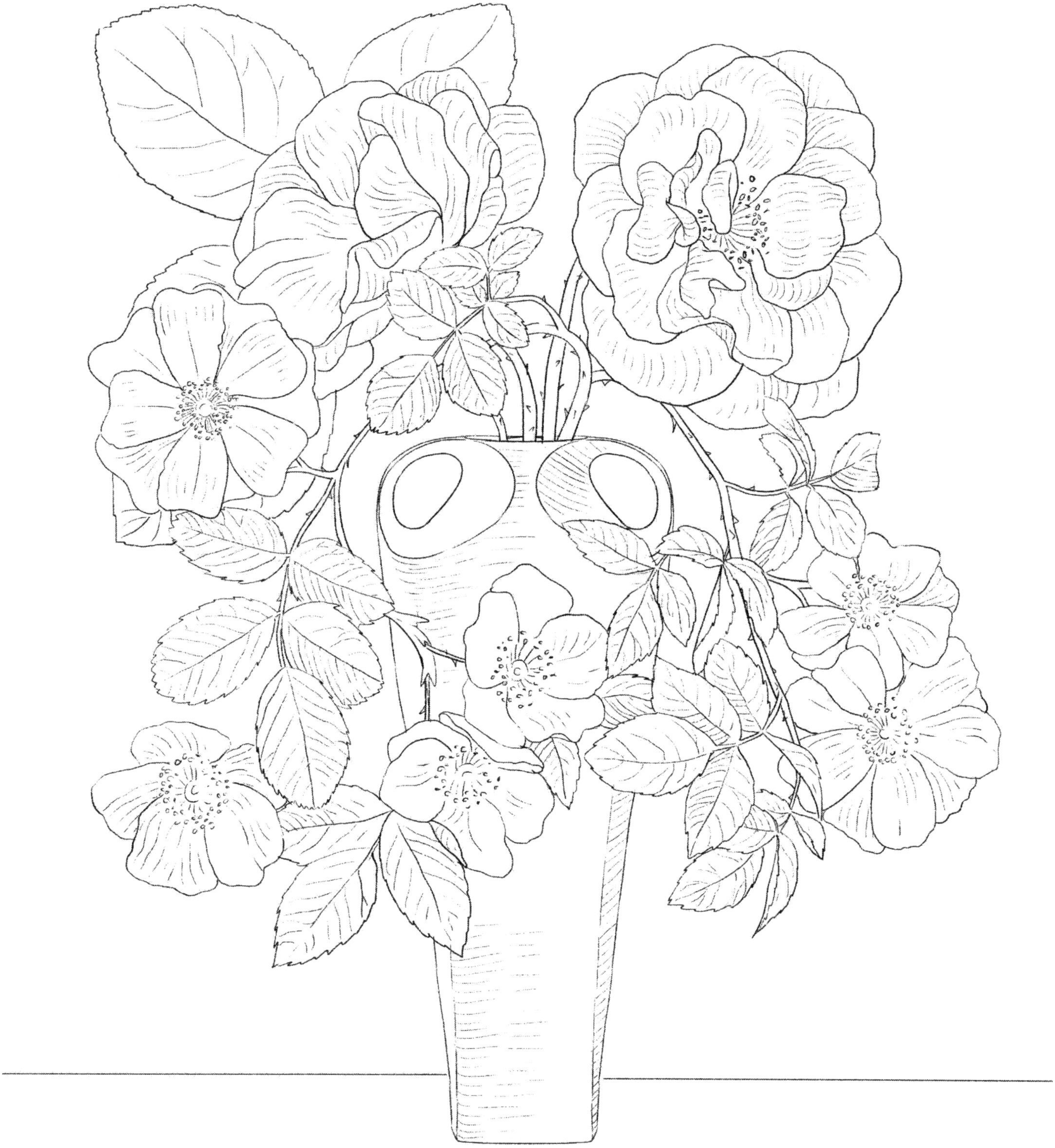

*Tulips*

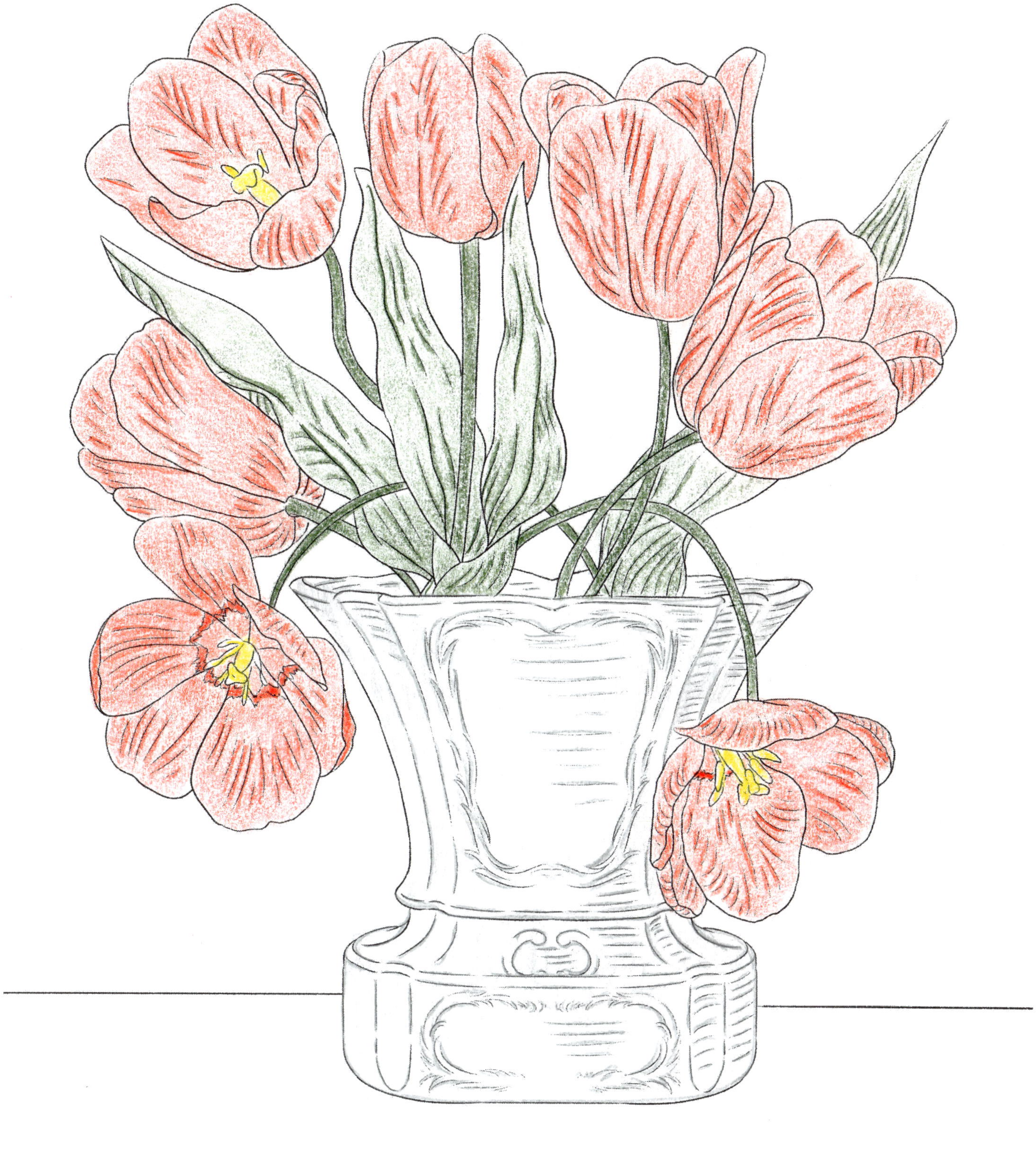

# Campanula Isophylla
## (Italian Bell Flower)

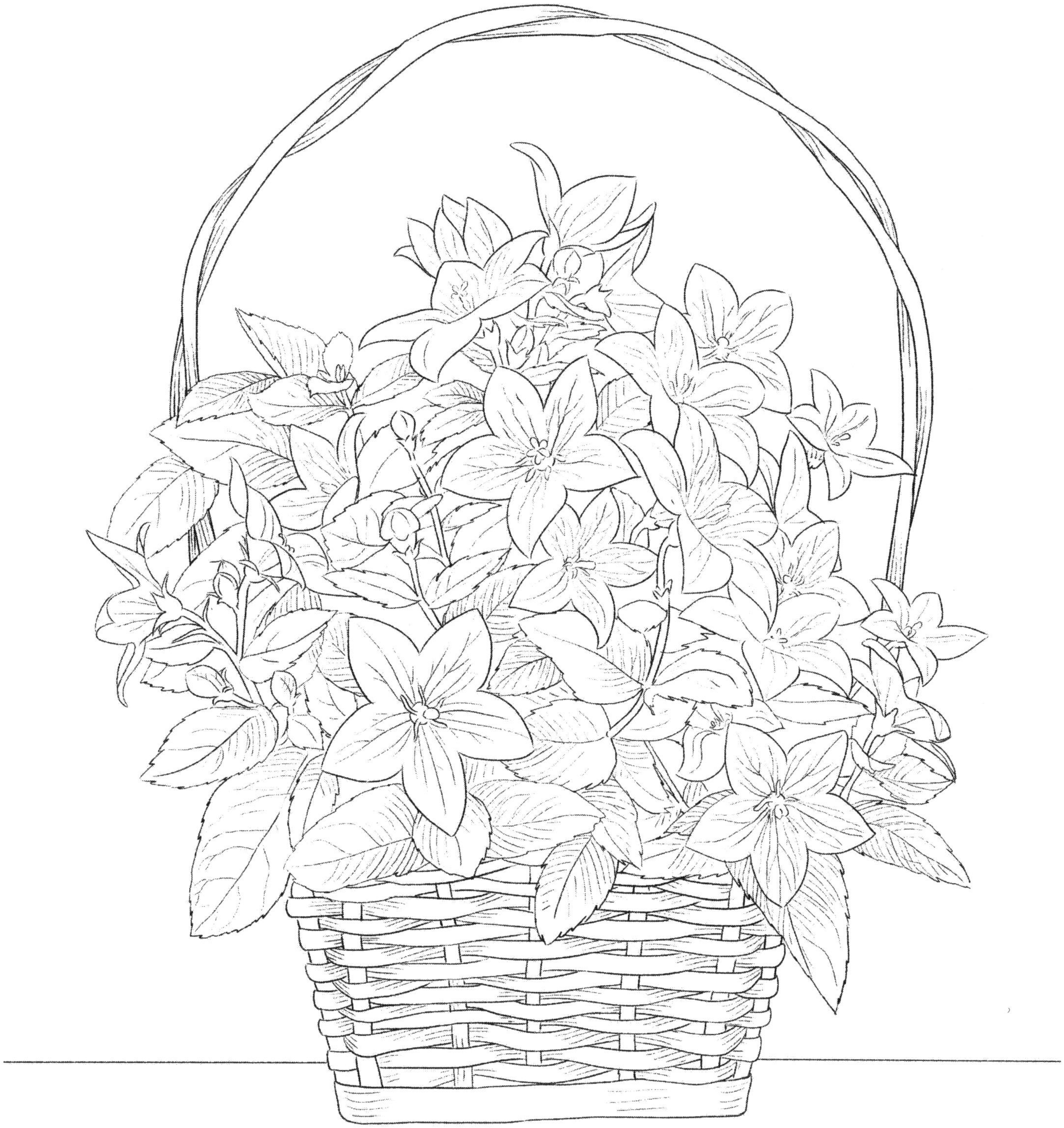

*Alcea Rosea*
*Hollyhock*

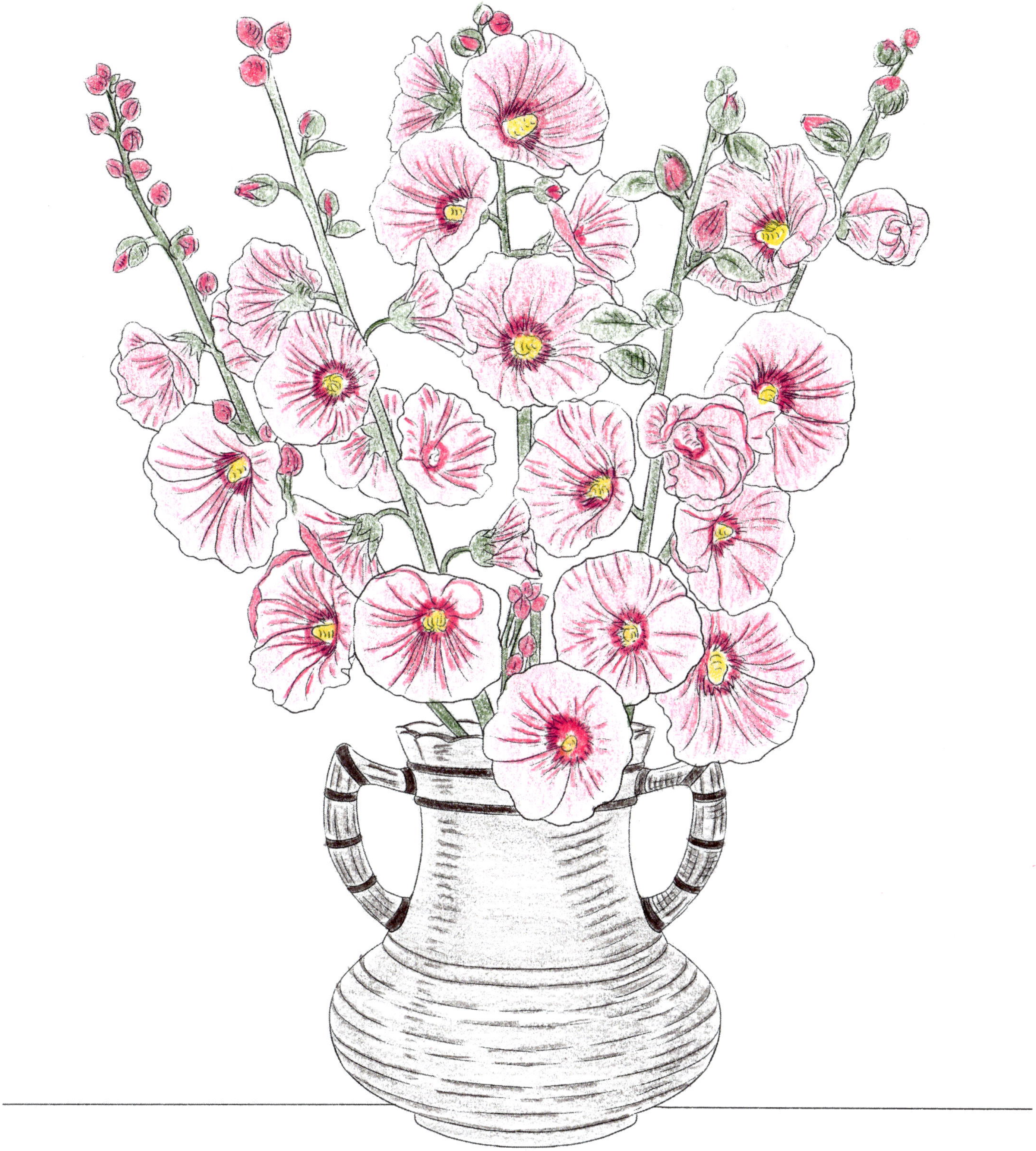

Made in the USA
Columbia, SC
08 November 2019